My Mistress' Eyes

Peter Leigh

Published in association with
The Basic Skills Agency

Hodder & Stoughton

A MEMBER OF THE HODDER HEADLINE GROUP

Acknowledgements
Illustrations: Mike Bell / Ian Fleming Associates.
Cover: Lee Stinton / Organisation.

Orders: please contact Bookpoint Ltd, 39 Milton Park, Abingdon, Oxon OX14 4TD. Telephone: (44) 01235 400414, Fax: (44) 01235 400454. Lines are open from 9.00–6.00, Monday to Saturday, with a 24 hour message answering service. Email address: orders@bookpoint.co.uk

British Library Cataloguing in Publication Data
A catalogue record for this title is available from The British Library

ISBN 0 340 72100 6

First published 1998
Impression number   10 9 8 7 6 5 4 3 2
Year   2002 2001 2000 1999 1998

Copyright © 1998 Peter Leigh

Typeset by Fakenham Photosetting Ltd, Fakenham, Norfolk.
Printed in Great Britain for Hodder & Stoughton Educational, a division of Hodder Headline Plc, 338 Euston Road, London NW1 3BH by Athenaeum Press Ltd, Gateshead, Tyne & Wear.

About the play

The People

- **Gary**
- **Laura**
- **Mark**
- **Rachel**
- **Jasmine**
- **Tony**

They are all from a Year 9 class.

What's Happening

All the characters come crashing into a classroom.

Gary	I want the teacher's chair.
	I'm in charge,
	so I have to sit at the front.
Mark	Why are you in charge?
Gary	Because Miss said so,
	and because I'm so cool!
Rachel	Oh he is, isn't he, Jaz? So cool!
Jasmine	So ace!
Rachel	And fit!
Jasmine	And tasty!
Jasmine/Rachel	And MODEST!
Gary	All right fans,
	I can't help being so great.
	I was just born that way.
Mark	It's a shame he was born at all.
Laura	What are we doing here?
	I don't want to be here at all.

Tony	Yes! Why us?
	What have we done?
Gary	Come on. You heard what
	Miss said.
	She'll be back in five minutes.
	We've got to make a start on
	this poem.
Tony	What poem?
	I don't want to read a stupid old
	poem.
Laura	I hate poems.
Gary	Look, all we've got to do is read
	this poem, and work out what
	it means.
	It shouldn't take too long.
Mark	Come on then.
	Read it out.
	Let's hear it!
Gary	What do you mean?
Mark	What do you mean 'What do I
	mean?'
	Read it out loud,
	so we can all hear it.

Gary	Who? Me?
Mark	Yes, you!
Gary	Why me?
Mark	(*laughs*) Because you're in charge.
	You said so.
Rachel	And you're so cool!
Gary	All right, all right.
	I'll read the first line.
	Right then.
	Quiet everybody!

Silence

Mark	Come on then!
Gary	All right.
	I'm coming.
	Don't rush me!

Silence

Jasmine/Rachel   (*singing*)
        Why are we waiting?

Gary   I said I'm coming.
        Just be patient ...
        Right then ... Ready.

        (*slowly reads*)

        'My – mis – tress' – eyes – are
        – nothing – like – the sun.'

        Silence

        Right! There we are then.

        Silence

Gary	OK?
Tony	What does it mean?
Gary	What do you mean, 'What does it mean?'
	It's obvious isn't it?

Silence

	Well, 'My mistress' eyes,' ...
	that is, the eyes of my mistress ...
	'are nothing like' ...
	are not anything like ...
	'the sun.'
	Well,
	they're not anything like the sun.
Mark	You mean they're more like the Mirror.
Rachel	Or the Star.
Jasmine	Or the Daily Mail.

Mark	Laura likes a daily male, don't you Laura?
Laura	Oh Ha! Ha! Very funny!
Gary	No, it doesn't mean that, you idiot!
Mark	Well, what is it then?
Gary	Well … it's … it's …
Tony	And what's a mistress?
Mark	It's what MPs have, isn't it?
Rachel	Isn't it what they used to call teachers? Lady teachers?
Jasmine	Oh great! 'The eyes of my old lady teacher are nothing like the Daily Mail!'

Laughter

Mark	Nice one, Jaz!

Laura	No, no! It doesn't mean that at all. He just means his girlfriend. And the sun's meant to be bright and shiny, so he's just saying that his girlfriend's eyes aren't bright and shiny like the sun.

(*Pause while this sinks in*)

Gary	Oh, right then!
Tony	Well, my eyes are nothing like the sun either.
Gary	He's not talking about your eyes, stupid. He's talking about his girlfriend's.
Mark	Never mind, Tony. I think your eyes are just like the sun – all red and hot.

Gary	Let's just get on shall we!
	(reads slowly)
	'Coral – is – far – more – red – than – her – lips – red.'
Tony	What's coral?
Mark	It's a bookies, isn't it?
Rachel	Are you sure it isn't 'Carol'?
Jasmine	Or 'Kerri'?
Mark	Or curry?
Laura	Isn't it where they go scuba-diving on the TV? With sharks and angel-fish?
Rachel	And spear guns?
Jasmine	And snorkels?
Mark	Don't be dirty!
Laura	The coral reef! That's what it's called.
Tony	But what is coral?
Laura	Well, I suppose it's a sort of shell.

Tony	And what colour is it?
Laura	Well, I suppose it's a sort of red.
	Yes, that's it!
	He's saying that her lips aren't
	as red as coral.
Gary	Oh! Right then!
	'My girlfriend's eyes aren't
	bright and shiny,
	and her lips aren't very red.'
	I thought he was meant to like
	this girl.
	What's next then?
	'If – snow – be – white, – why –
	then –
	her – breasts – are – dun.'
Tony	That's rude!
Mark	Hey, this poem is sexy.
	He's talking about her ...
Laura	(*quickly*)
	Don't say it!
	Don't say that word!
	I hate that word.

Mark	What word?
Laura	What you were just going to say.
Mark	What's wrong with it?
Laura	I just hate it, that's all!
Mark	It's what everyone says.
Laura	That's it!
	It's crude, and it's mean!
	You only say it when you want
	to put us down.
	It's a horrible little word,
	and if you use it,
	that means you're a horrible
	little person!
Rachel	Right on, Laura!
Mark	I'm not a horrible little person.
Laura	Well, use another word then.
Tony	The poem says 'breasts'.
Mark	'Breasts' sounds stupid!

Jasmine	Boobs, use boobs.
Rachel	Yes, I like boobs.
Gary	I like boobs too.

(groans from the others)

	All right, all right.
	It was just a joke.
	Look Laura, are you happy
	with boobs?
Laura	I suppose so!
	At least it's better than what
	Mark was going to say.
Gary	Right then.
	So this means her boobs are dun.
Tony	Done what?
Rachel	Done in?
Jasmine	Done up?
Mark	Underdone?
	Overdone?
	What have they done?

Laura	No, it's not that sort of 'done'.
	Look, it's all opposites.
	It says 'if – snow – be – white'
	so if snow is all clean and white,
	then her boobs must be the
	opposite.
Tony	What is the opposite?
Laura	Well, dull and dirty I suppose.
Gary	Well, that's not very nice is it?
	'My girlfriend's boobs are
	dull and dirty!'
	And look what it says next –
	'If – hair – be – wires,
	– black – wires – grow – on – her
	– head.'
	He's saying her hair is like wire.
	So altogether we've got:
	'My girlfriend's eyes aren't very
	bright,
	her lips aren't very red,
	her boobs are all dirty-looking,
	and she's got hair like brillo pads!'

Rachel	Charming, I must say!
Jasmine	If my boyfriend said that to me, I'd smash his face in.
Gary	Lucky for him he can't talk then!
Mark	I don't know. I think this Shakespeare's got something. This sounds just like the girls in this class.
Rachel/Jasmine	Ha, ha! Very funny!
Tony	Good one, Mark!
Laura	No – look, he's not really serious. He's just trying not to say all the rubbish men usually come out with. You know the sort of stuff I mean.

(*in a posh voice*)
'Your hair is a golden waterfall.'

Rachel	'Your eyes are twin pools of darkness.'
Jasmine	'Your skin is like a velvet glove.'
Laura	'Your teeth are like stars.'
Rachel/Jasmine	(*laughing*)
	They come out at night.
Laura	See?
	All that romantic rubbish.
	The stuff you read on
	Valentines.
Mark	You must know some funny men.
	'Your hair is a golden waterfall!'
	Sounds stupid!
	I've never said anything like that to a girl in my life.

Rachel	We've heard what you say to a girl …
Jasmine	… and we wouldn't want to repeat it!
Laura	It's just that Shakespeare is trying to be more honest, more real. Look at the next lines – 'I – have – seen – roses – damasked – red – and – white, But – no – such –roses –see – I – in – her – cheeks.'
Tony	What's damasked mean?

Laura	Well, I don't know.
	But you can tell what he means.
	He's saying that her cheeks aren't like roses.
	He's seen roses – they're pink and white,
	and her skin's not like that at all.
Gary	Well, what about the next bit?
	'And – in – some – perfumes – there – is – more – delight
	Than – in – the – breath – that – from – my – mistress – reeks.'
Tony	Is he saying that her breath smells?
Mark	That's a bit cheeky, isn't it?
Rachel	I mean it's one thing trying to be honest, but if he's saying she's got dog breath …
Laura	Well, I suppose he might be going a bit far there,
	but he's only saying that perfumes
	smell a bit nicer than she does.

Jasmine	Oh I don't know, I think I might prefer smelly breath to that stuff you boys throw over yourselves.
Gary	What do you mean?
Jasmine	Well, take Mark here. When he comes back from games, you can't go near him – not that I'd want to, I mean – you can smell him a mile off. All that cheap perfume.
Mark	What do you mean, cheap perfume? It's really expensive – 50p a bottle!
Jasmine	Yes, but even at a whole 50p a bottle, you're not meant to use it all at once.
Rachel	And you're meant to be clean first. You don't just spray it on top of what's already there!

Mark   Look, I don't smell, all right?
If anyone round here smells
it's you!

Rachel   I don't smell! I wash! Not like you!

Gary   All right, all right!
             Let's stop shouting
             or we'll be here all night.
             Let's read the next bit –
             'I – love – to – hear – her – speak,
             – yet – well – I – know
             That – music – hath – a – far –
             more – pleasing – sound.'
             That's pretty clear, isn't it?
             It means I like talking to her,
             and listening to her voice,
             but I know music sounds
             much nicer.

Mark   If he likes listening to girls talk,
             he ought to be round here.
             That's all they do all day long
             – yak, yak, yak!

Rachel/Jasmine   Oh, shut up!

Mark   And as for music,
             what about that stuff that
             Laura likes?

Tony	It sounds like frogs croaking.
Mark	I thought it was frogs croaking.
Gary	Oh come on! Shut it, you two.
	I want to get this finished!
	'I – grant – I – never – saw
	– a – goddess – go,'
Rachel	Go where? Go home?
Jasmine	Go to work? Go to bed?
	Where do goddesses go?
Tony	They live in heaven, don't they?
	In the sky?
Gary	Yes, that's it, because the
	next line says –
	'My – mistress – when – she –
	walks – treads
	– on – the – ground.'
	So he's saying that he hasn't
	seen a goddess,
	but he knows his girlfriend
	isn't one,
	because she walks on the ground
	and doesn't fly through the air.

Laura	And he's not going to pretend she's one either.
Gary	What do you mean?
Laura	Well, it's all about pretending, isn't it. Men pretend women are amazingly beautiful.
Mark	Why?
Laura	Why do you think It's obvious, isn't it? Just to flatter them. So they can get off with them. But he says he's not going to pretend, he's going to be honest.
Gary	Oh! ... Right! ... Well, what do the last lines say then? 'And – yet, – by – heaven, – I – think – my – love – as – rare As – any – she – belied – by – false – compare.' Well, what does that mean then?

Mark	Dunno!
Tony	Haven't a clue!
Rachel	No idea!
Jasmine	Search me!
Laura	(*excited*)

Oh, don't you see? Don't you see?
He really loves her.
He really cares.
And he cares for her, herself,
as she really is.
Not some mushy picture in a
magazine.
He knows she'll never be on TV.
She hasn't got perfect hair,
perfect face,
perfect figure.

Jasmine   She's not like the girls on
Baywatch.

Laura   Yes! But he doesn't care.
That's all false in any case.
He really loves her for what she is,
stinky breath and all.
And he thinks his love is
something rare,
something fine and wonderful ...

(*falters*)

... well, that's what I think,
anyway.

Tony   You're right Laura,
something fine and wonderful.

Rachel   I think it's lovely.

Jasmine   It makes me go all wobbly
inside.

Gary   Let's read the whole thing
shall we?

All together   (*slowly*)

'My mistress' eyes are nothing
   like the sun.
Coral is far more red
   than her lips red.
If snow be white, why then
   her breasts are dun,
If hairs be wires, black wires
   grow on her head.
I have seen roses damasked
   red and white,
But no such roses see I
   in her cheeks.
And in some perfumes
   there is more delight
Than in the breath that from
   my mistress reeks.
I love to hear her speak,
   yet well I know
That music hath a far
   more pleasing sound.

I grant that I never saw
   a goddess go,
My mistress, when she walks,
   treads on the ground.
And yet, by heaven, I think
   my love as rare
As any she belied with
   false compare.'

(*Pause*)

Gary   Wicked, eh?

Laura   What do you think, Mark?

Mark   Well, I think you're right Laura, but there's just one question bugging me?

Laura   What's that then?

Mark   What's wrong with the girls on Baywatch?
(*Groans, laughter, sounds of **Mark** being thumped*)